Between the TREATMENTS

OUR JOURNEY THROUGH CANCER TREATMENT

KENNETH, ETHEL & SETH ANTOINE

KESZA Publishing LLC
P.O. Box 1295
Marrero, La. 70073

ISBN: 978-0-9963430-6-0

TABLE OF CONTENTS

INTRODUCTION

What do you do when life throws an unexpected curve ball? What do you do when the curveball that life has just thrown you seems unhittable? How do you handle it when you're faced with problems that seem unsolvable? How do you handle life when you're faced with issues not caused by you? Well, just such a problem and issue happened to us. In this book, we will tell you about the year 2013 when our life was turned upside down. We will take you on the journey of the day-to-day life of our family as we dealt with our son being diagnosed with cancer. It is our desire that as you read this book you will find answers to some of these questions. It is our hopes and desires that the words on the pages of this book will leap into your heart and help you to navigate through life issues. It is the story of our precious son Zachary Isaac Antoine and the lives of three of us as we had to make quick decisions, make unwanted changes, and handle everything that was thrown at us unexpectedly. We believe that this book can help not just people dealing with cancer but any sickness and any other problems that life can throw at you. You will be able to apply the principles, the wisdom, and experiences that we share to hopefully apply them to what you are dealing with in your life. Get ready to go on a journey of the family that lived life *Between the Treatments.*

CHAPTER ONE

ZACKIE

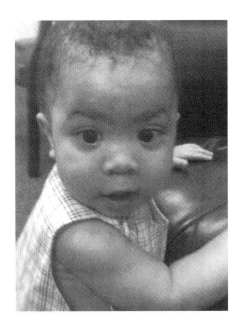

Zachary Isaac Antoine

October 29, 2012 – August 2, 2014

You never forget the day your child was diagnosed with Stage 4 Liver Cancer; it was October 30, 2013. Likewise, you never forget the day your child breathes his last breath and passes away; it was August 2, 2014. You never forget them because they are the days that Zackie's life and ours were changed forever. As parents, when our children are born, it's only natural for us to believe they're born to become a part of the family. But, when Zackie was born, we knew early on we were chosen to be a part of his journey.

Zackie was born on October 29, 2012. He was an amazing little boy with lots of energy and determination. There was something about Zackie that would help you to understand just how special he was. Maybe it was his big brown eyes that would radiate love and kindness. Maybe it was his long softly curled eyelashes that women would always compliment him on. Maybe it was his big cheesy smile that would instantly brighten your day.

While Zackie did possess all those features; what made him special was that he didn't let cancer beat him.

Zackie was 12 months old when he was diagnosed and 21 months old when he passed away, but what happened within those ten months between diagnosis and death was nothing short of remarkable. Zackie displayed incredible strength and a *never quit* determination like you wouldn't believe was possible in a child his age. While receiving at times the most intense chemotherapy treatment, he never stopped smiling and he never stopped fighting. There were days when he physically could not stand up, but that didn't stop Zackie. He would spend hours holding on to furniture moving from one place to the next—this was how he moved around.

Zackie was truly an inspiration to all who witnessed him with grace, dignity and a never quit attitude—enduring the most difficult time of his life. He lived his life full of love, laughter and happiness. His story and legacy are the message of inspiration and determination. Be inspired to live! Be determined to make it!

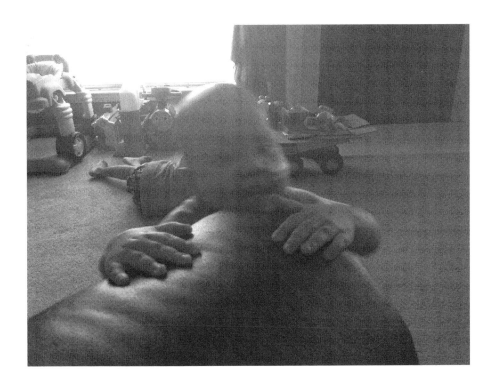

CHAPTER TWO

THE ENEMY CALLED HEPATOBLASTOMA

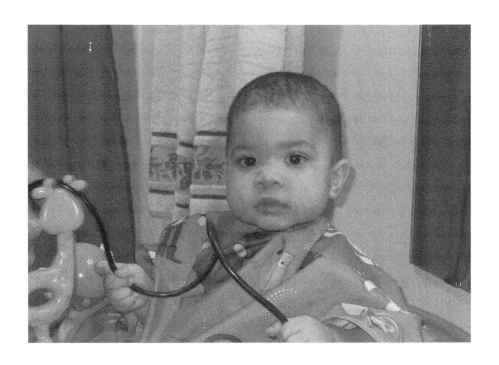

I will never forget that day. It was October 30, 2013. We had just celebrated Zackie's one year birthday the day before. We were excited to see him growing up so nicely. We had plans for him. It was our intention to get him ready to go to school with his older brother Seth. We laid our plans out nicely. First, we had to get him potty-trained, second, make sure he was able to walk securely on his own, and then off to school with his brother whom he watched exit the car every morning, and couldn't wait to see him later that day. We took him to his one-year annual checkup on that day that would change our lives forever.

Just like every school morning, the house was busy getting Seth ready for school, but this morning we had to make sure Zackie was presentable for his doctor's appointment. We dropped Seth off and headed for Zackie's appointment. We were going to enjoy the day with him. We had plans of going to lunch and maybe strolling through the shopping center or just walking in the park. We pulled up to the doctor's office and did our usual routine. We waited in the lobby for his name to be called. There we were, just the three of us, talking and playing with our growing baby. They called his name and we went to the room after having him checked in and weighed. My wife began to take pictures like she normally did. I held him and bounced him on my knee. He was happy as usual to be with both of us. Then the doctor entered the room. She asked us the normal questions, how are we doing? How is the baby? Are there any concerns? What brings us in today? We told her that we noticed Zachary's stomach was a little harder than usual. She asked us how long it has been that way. We then reminded her that we were just in her office two weeks ago and it wasn't like this. She laid him down and began her examination.

We then noticed that her expression began to change. She had this deep concern and worry that clouded her face. She turned to us and said to us to go directly to the children's hospital! As she was examining him, she noticed that there was a mass on his stomach that concerned her. Before we left for the hospital she measured the mass and again directed us go directly to the hospital. Trying not to panic, we picked him up and headed to the hospital. Because we are people of faith, we began to confess that nothing was wrong with our child as we made our way to the hospital.

Once we arrived, the doctors were already aware of Zackie's situation. They began to run all kinds of tests on him and asked us what seemed like a million questions. This seemed like the longest day of our lives.

We could tell by the expressions on the doctors' faces and the way they were talking that there was something awfully wrong here. They didn't want to tell us anything concrete, but we knew something

wasn't right. They told us that they wanted to wait on the lab results before they could tell us anything for certain.

I remember we decided that I would pick Seth up from school as my wife stayed with Zackie. The entire way to my son's school I prayed and prayed for my child's healing. Not knowing what we were facing, I believed for total healing and restoration—no matter what it was.

THE CALL

I was on my way back to the hospital when that call came in. My wife called to tell me what the doctors were trying to do. They had decided to put a port in because, in their eyes, they were up against the clock.

I insistently said no! Why a port? What are you saying? All of my manners were gone. I began to insist that they tell me something.

Why do you want to put a port in my son if you don't know what's wrong with him? I'm not claiming that God forbidden C-word!

They began to explain to us that they strongly believed that our precious little baby had cancer, and they felt like it was really advanced. So to get a jumpstart on the process, they wanted to put the port in while they were getting a biopsy.

I didn't know what to say, I couldn't put it all together... it was too much, too suddenly, too soon. What are you really telling us?

After listening and talking, we decided that no matter what he needed, we were going to make sure he had it. I told the doctor ok. I then had to turn around and go home to get some clothes for the night, and also feed my son Seth—all while not trying to scare him with my concerns.

I can remember running through the house trying to pack a bag for what I hoped would be one night. When I returned to the hospital, we were informed that it would be two or three days before they would get the biopsy results back.

It was the longest three days of our lives. I can remember looking at my precious little boy as he had no idea what was happening. The whole day seemed like a nightmare. I can remember watching the concerned faces of everyone who would enter the room. Even though they didn't have any concrete news back from the lab, it was obvious that they knew what they were dealing with.

Everything since that call was on the fast track. Doctor after doctor, nurse after nurse entered Zackie's room all night checking vitals and doing their jobs. I must tell you; it was the longest few days in my entire life.

THE MEETING

When the results of his biopsy came in, the doctors scheduled a meeting with us to go over their finding. As you may realize; our hearts and minds were all over the place.

Because of my faith in my God; I didn't allow myself to even say that C-word or think of the possibility of what we were about to face. I stayed focused on my child and made sure that he was as comfortable as possible.

I could tell by their demeanor that this was going to be very difficult. With sad looks and distress on their faces; they began to tell us that our son had Cancer.

I can remember as I sat there watching them, their lips were moving but for a minute I couldn't hear anything they were saying. I stared at them with this intense look as to say; Don't say it! Don't say it! But to no avail... it came out of their mouths in no uncertain terms. Your son has cancer.

My heart dropped! My emotions were all over the place. I didn't want to hear that word, nor did I want to bare the thoughts of someone that I love having to deal with cancer—someone so very young.

THE ENEMY

It has a name. It invaded our lives. The enemy you hear about but hope to never have to personally deal with.

The doctors pulled out this chart and began to show us his labs and the results of what they believed to be cancer of the liver. Its name is Hepatoblastoma. Hepatoblastoma became our enemy.

All I knew was this wasn't a friend of ours. This thing that has invaded our little baby must be destroyed at any cost and by all means necessary.

LIVER CANCER

The liver is an organ located in the upper right side of the abdomen, under the rib cage. The liver is important in removing toxin from the blood, producing blood clotting proteins, and helping the body to digest food and absorb medicine. Liver cancer occurs when a liver cell develops a series of mutations or mistakes that allows it to grow without the usual controls and to form cancerous tumors.

Hepatoblastoma occurs most frequently in infants or very young children. Our son was only one year old when we learned of this enemy invading his body.

The enemy that has attacked our son has finally been identified. It had a name but no face. We couldn't see it! We couldn't rip its head off! We couldn't take a weapon and shoot it! It had a name but to us... we didn't know anything about it.

They handed us a folder full of information about this new enemy to learn what it was. I must admit; I didn't want to hear or learn anything about this awful thing that has attacked my baby. But I also knew that if we're going to wage war against this new enemy, we had to become more knowledgeable about it. I can remember that I had this mindset that I didn't even want to dignify this enemy by learning how to pronounce its name. I wouldn't even allow it to roll off my lips. You see; all I could think about was what happened? Where did I go wrong? How did I miss such a big enemy? How could I have let my family down like this? I always considered myself a protector of all I love. No one would ever come into my space or home and attack anyone I was responsible for... But there it was; not only did it invade my home; but it had the audacity to attack the smallest person in my home. This enemy had to go!

We began to learn as much as possible about this enemy. Where did it come from? How does it function? What makes it tick? What is its weaknesses, and finally, how can we destroy it! As we continued to talk to the doctors about treatments, they decided that the best course of action would be chemotherapy. They laid out this plan of chemo that would give him the best chance to beat this enemy. We had to wrap our minds around all of the side effects that was possible with such an aggressive treatment. You see; Zackie had just celebrated his first birthday and I cut his hair for the first time and he was very handsome. The doctors informed us that one of the first side effects could possibly be hair loss, and as expected; he lost his beautiful head of hair.

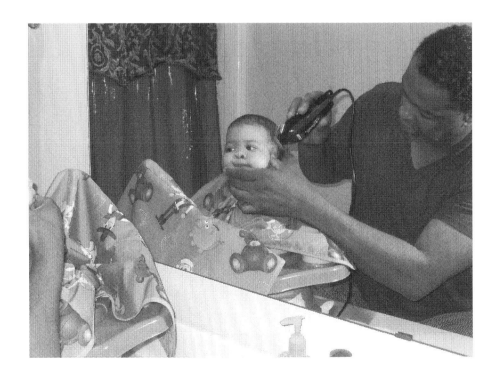

I can remember it like yesterday watching him rub his head as to say; where is my hair daddy? I viewed it as this enemy winning the first round of what was going to be the fight of our life. It hurt me to my heart to see him confused about one minute having a head full of hair, to no hair at all. The doctors informed us that these side effects were not all bad because it simply meant that the treatment was working, but from where I stood, it looked like the enemy was winning. I viewed it like this, don't hurt my child! Don't take anything from him! Leave him alone! Leave him just like you found him! I also realized that I had to do what I did, and that was to fight the faith fight for my child while allowing the doctors to do what they knew to do, and that was treating my son.

Little did we know, we were on a journey that would change our lives forever. It started what we now call "Between the Treatments."

Between the treatments would be our life moments when we would look forward to enjoying each other without being at the doctor's office or the hospital. It was between the treatments that our lives were normalized to some degree.

CHAPTER THREE

FROM A FATHER'S PERSPECTIVE

MY FEELINGS

I want to start this chapter by explaining how I felt as a father seeing his child fight for his little life. I think sometimes as people of faith we tend to act as if nothing bothers us. I believe we can do people a great deal of harm by hiding our true feelings when things happen to us.

I consider myself to be a strong man. I normally don't allow my emotions to show publicly. You see, I was raised to believe that real men didn't show their emotions. We were always expected to be strong. I actually took pride in the fact that no one was ever going to see me sweat.

I broke my ankle when I was in middle school, and I didn't even cry. The first girl I liked didn't know I was alive, but I didn't let my feelings show. I've been through so much pain in my life, but I handled all of it. Until this enemy showed up to hurt someone I loved! My emotions were all over the place. I was angered, hurt, sad, and confused. I couldn't believe that something you read about or watched someone else deal with was happening to me.

I take being a father extremely serious. I was going to be the kind of father that didn't miss anything. I went to every doctor's appointment, meeting, test, and anything else that concerned my family. I was the protector of my family. I took my job as the man of the house serious. I knew the kind of world we live in, so

I made sure to take extra precaution when it came to my family.

I learned this from my father, who to me, was a strong man. He provided for his family and never complained. I watched him get up early and go to work so he could provide everything we needed. I always felt like I was going to be the same kind of man I witnessed my father being—strong, a provider, and a great teacher. I knew I had to come up with a game plan for our new normal, as we navigated life between the treatments.

STORY FROM THE PAST

I remember when I was young living with my parents, I would be the brother who fought off anyone that messed with my family. My father would take me to the garage and show me how to fight. He really thought that I had a natural gift when it came to boxing. I really enjoyed those times my father and I spent working on the punching bag and jumping rope. My father was an avid boxing fan. He really liked watching boxing matches. So whenever some kid in the neighborhood would try to mess with us, I would be the one that handled it. I grew up protecting those that I love. I grew confidence in the fact that no one would ever hurt anybody in my life. I really felt like I could protect my loved ones from any seen or unseen intruder.

THE FAITH FIGHT

Then it happened. I was faced with an enemy I've never met before, nor could I beat it with my boxing skills. I couldn't even see the intruder. The level of emotion that ran through my mind and body was never felt before. I didn't know how to process it. I've consoled many people in my life before, but here I was sitting in the other chair. It was my turn now. How would I handle life between the treatments? How would I deal with this enemy? I knew we were in for the fight of our lives, and it would be important for us to fight together and not allow anyone else to divide us. We had to bring as much normalcy as possible to this impossible situation for our sons. We could not afford to lose ourselves in this fight and allow our family to be destroyed. This fight was real, and we had to be ready.

I hope my transparency will help you to realize that you are a person with natural feelings also. It's not healthy to go through life feeling like you have to be strong all the time. I believe God has surrounded us with friends and family members to help us through difficult times we will face in life.

MY FAITH

My faith in my Lord and Savior Jesus Christ is what got me through the most difficult time of my life. My faith teaches me to cast all of my cares on the One who truly cares for me. I realize that everyone may not believe in the same God I do, and some might even consider what I'm saying as weakness, but this is my story and I'm sticking to it.

I have been a believer in Jesus Christ for as long as I can remember. I believe that had it not been for my faith in my Lord and Savior Jesus Christ, I truly don't know where I would be. My faith teaches me that we do all that we can in the natural and we depend on the Lord for the supernatural.

It was in this difficult time of my life that I can truly thank God for the strength to make it through, and to be a source of strength for my family in one of the greatest struggles of our life.

As I sit here and think about it today as I write this book, I can only marvel at the fact that God provided the strength I needed to even be able now to pen this book.

I thank my God that I was even able to go through such a hard time in my life. I give God all of the credit for all of the things that He had done in and through my life.

Later on in this book I will talk more about God's grace. It is in and through this grace that me and my family were allowed to make it through one of the roughest seasons of our life, and to be able to navigate life between the treatments.

THE VISIT

I can remember it like it was yesterday. I was in the room with Zackie and it was nighttime. I had just changed his diaper, cleaned, fed and put him to sleep. I turned the light off and sat down in the chair on the left side of his bed.

I began to pray and talk to God honestly about how I was feeling about all of this. I could hear laughter and joy that

I've never heard before; it sounded like it was a bunch of kids running up the hallway laughing and playing. I found this extremely strange because at this time of night I knew the kids wouldn't be playing in the hallways. And then it hit me, I was still in the hospital and little children on this floor were not running, laughing and playing. I stood up, opened the door and looked out and to my surprise no one, not a single soul was in the hallway. What was this that I was hearing? I know that I was not losing my mind, and then I heard it again—children running, laughing and playing—with a sense of joy I've never heard before, with such a sense of peace I've never experienced.

I sat there understanding that God had allowed me to experience His peace in the midst of such pain. As I sat there not knowing exactly what was going on, it was evident that heaven had invaded not just the room but the hallways. I can remember that while I laid there listening to the sound of children playing the door swung open, but no one was there. Shortly thereafter the nurse came into the room looking like she just saw a ghost. She asked me how did I know that she was about to come to the room? I said I had no idea she was coming. She said someone opened the door, but she saw that I was sitting down.

I then understood that the presence of the Lord was right there with me and my precious son.

He allowed me to hear little children in heaven filled with joy and peace, and that His presence was right there.

Such a calmness came over me that I cannot begin to explain. I just looked at the nurse, smiled and knew in my heart that I was not alone—that not only was the presence of God in my room, but He brought little children with Him.

I could only imagine that not only myself, but other little children in that hospital must entertain angels in the midst of the worst season of their lives. What an awesome God we serve!

I believe that having faith in my Lord and Savior Jesus Christ is wisdom. I don't believe that having faith is weakness. I am a firm believer that it is in and through my Lord and Savior Jesus Christ that I made it through one of the roughest seasons of my life.

I could not have ever imagined going through something like the transitioning of my son without Him.

WORDS OF ENCOURAGEMENT

Let me encourage all of you that are reading this book to find your strength in the Lord.

I understand what you're going through. I understand the depths of your pain. I understand sitting in a chair in the hospital room, watching the walls, listening to the nurses, listening to the doctors, walking around and feeling as if nobody knows what you're dealing with.

If I have to credit anything for our ability to make it through one of the hardest times of our life, one of the hardest seasons we've ever had to go through, it would be because of our faith in our Savior.

I thank my God that He is a God that's right there at the lowest point. He is a God in the valley as well as a God on the mountain. He is a God with you between the treatments.

He is with you at your lowest point and He is also with you at your highest point.

I am a pastor in the church, so I can understand. I've spent many years walking down this road with others, I've had to comfort so many people going through what I had to go through.

It is my prayer as you read this book, that it will strengthen your faith, help you to find your faith, or even pull on the strength of my faith.

Always remember this, there's nothing that you're going through right now that someone else has not dealt with. You are not alone in this fight. We are praying with and for you.

I want you to continue to read the rest of this book and draw from our strength to help you deal with what you're going through, and to be encouraged as you deal with life between the treatments.

CHAPTER FOUR

FROM A MOTHER'S PERSPECTIVE

A MOTHER'S PERSPECTIVE

You never forget the day your child was diagnosed with Stage 4 Liver Cancer, it was October 30, 2013; the day after his first birthday. Likewise, you never forget the day your child breathes his last breath and passes away; it was August 2, 2014. You never forget them because they are the days that Zackie's life and ours were changed forever. As parents, when our children are born, it's only natural for us to believe they're born to become a part of the family. But when Zackie was born, we knew early on we were chosen to be a part of his journey.

Zackie was 12 months old when he was diagnosed and 21 months old when he passed away; but what happened within those ten months between diagnosis and death was nothing short of remarkable.

Zackie displayed incredible strength and a never quit determination like you wouldn't believe was possible in a child his age.

While receiving at times the most intense chemotherapy treatment, he never stopped smiling and he never stopped fighting. There were days when he physically could not stand up because his little baby tummy was the size of a kid's basketball, but that didn't stop Zackie.

He would hold on to furniture moving from one place to the next, this was how he moved around. He didn't let the fact that he couldn't walk stop him from getting around. After all, he had an older brother to chase after.

Zackie would spend hours building up the courage to let go of the furniture and walk without holding on to something—only for most of the time to end up on his bottom, but he never gave up. He was right back up trying it again and again, until one day he was able to come to a complete stand all by himself.

That's what we would call a "small victory." Although he never took a step without us supporting him, he never let the fact that he couldn't walk stop him from trying. Silently, he was my hero. I was truly inspired by his *never quit* anything... *finish everything* mentality.

Zackie was truly an inspiration to all of us who witnessed him with grace, dignity and a never quit attitude, enduring the most difficult time of his life.

There are no words to describe the pain you feel when your child dies. There are days that the pain hurts so bad it's hard to breathe.

But, we don't grieve as people without hope. Our hope is anchored in the solid rock—Jesus Christ. We know that Zackie is in heaven with God, Jesus and loved ones who have gone on before him. And we are assured that when we die we will see Zackie again. Until then, we take the memories we've made with him and cherish them in our hearts forever. We thank God for choosing us to be Zackie's family; his daddy, mama and brother. We thank God for loving Zackie through us. Boy, didn't we love him and still do. We thank God for an amazing little boy who lived his life full of love, laughter and happiness.

Between the treatments came to be a time of solace for us. It's the term my husband and I used to describe the time after a chemo cycle, a long hospital stay and discharge. It became the cycle of time where we were all together again as a family doing life and making memories.

When the chemo treatments were complete, our son was left with an extremely compromised immune system.

This was particularly hard for me because as a mom when your child is sick all you want is to help him feel better. Whenever he was discharged from the hospital that was a happy time because going home always made Zackie happy and that made me happy. During our between the treatment times, Zackie would slowly feel better and that made life feel normal. When life felt normal, my husband and I were able to rest, recharge and re-engage the battle.

Fast forward to ten months of chemo. The blood and platelet transfusions became more frequent, the CAT scans revealed the cancer was still spreading and Zackie was denied a liver transplant. My husband and I were ready and willing to give a portion of our livers to save our son's life... Still denied. Zackie's stomach was the size of a kid's basketball, imagine that. His little body was in excruciating pain and he was too young to tell me, mommy my tummy hurts, but I saw it in his eyes.

So for me, I knew that I couldn't get through this in my own strength, so I leaned on my Father God and my husband. I will tell you right away, my hope wasn't perfect as you will learn from my story and yours may not be either, but if you hang on to it and don't let go it will carry you through some difficult times.

This is my story of how I survived Zackie's Stage 4 Liver Cancer diagnosis, ten months of chemotherapy treatments, the passing of my son and how *hope* carried me through. This was without a doubt, the hardest time of my life, but *hope* led me out. It will lead you too, just grab it, hold on to it and never let go.

HANG ON TO HOPE

What do I do now? Now that the bad news, the unwanted diagnosis, or the fear that feels like a thousand pounds of pressure on your heart overwhelms you. If you have asked yourself this question, the answer is hope. Hope is your next step to take. You hope, hope some more, and continue to hope. Sounds too simple to be effective? Well, it isn't; it's just a matter of choice.

When you allow yourself to choose hope, then you will believe, and when you believe, well, that's called faith. In other words, hope is contagious. Yes, hope is contagious in a way that's good and healthy for your body, soul, and spirit. It will spread quickly and take over your entire body—when you draw back the curtains of fear and doubt and let hope shine through. Having hope will cause you to have faith and believe that you will live and not die. That you will make it through and past this moment of fear, pain and sorrow. So, at that very moment when you learn of the bad news, conquer the fear you're feeling by clinching tightly to hope as if it's someone you brought with you for support as you meet with the doctors. Hold hope's hand tightly, drawing faith from its power and ability to calm, soothe, and comfort any situation. Allow hope to become an unmovable and unshakable anchor for your belief and faith.

You see, I was exactly where you are right now. The receiver of bad news, though the diagnosis wasn't for me, it was for my 12-month-old son, Zachary. Tell me, what do you do with a Stage 4 Liver Cancer diagnosis for a 1-year-old? I'll tell you what. You hope, hope some more, and continue to hope. I say this because nothing prepares you on how to handle traumatic, life-changing experiences that interrupts your life—except your anchor of hope. At the very moment the diagnosis is given, instinctively the natural reaction is to fear, and its partner, sadness, moves in swiftly behind it. The dynamic duo's only job is to paralyze your faith with consuming thoughts of darkness and death. But, when you let down your anchor of hope, it firmly and securely plants your faith, trust, and belief in Jesus Christ and not in the diagnosis. When activated, hope acts as a force field that protects your faith from being infiltrated and ultimately destroyed. Instead of darkness and death, you are consumed with light and life. Tragedy strikes unexpectedly and swiftly, but with a foundation of hope you're able to walk in faith and belief. Here's how our traumatic experience began.

On October 30, 2013, my husband and I took Zackie to have his 1-year checkup. As the doctor was examining him, she felt a mass in his abdomen area. She recommended we have a CAT scan done to confirm her thoughts. Yes, the CAT scan revealed a large tumor in Zackie's liver, and it was aggressive and fast-growing. Our life, together as a family, was impacted by a Stage 4 Liver Cancer diagnosis that carried with it enough force to alter our course from normal to extremely difficult. In one day, we went from loving, living and having fun to chemo, blood and platelet transfusions and long hospital stays.

On that day, I clearly remember sitting in the emergency department in an exam room. The CAT scan was completed and we were waiting on the doctor to speak with us about the results. When the doctor came in, she sat on the exam table and began to introduce herself, she clearly told me that she was an oncology fellow. I'll never forget, she was wearing a football jersey, a jean skirt, a white lab coat, cowgirl boots and she was swinging her legs back and forth. She was being distracting with her cheery face, smile and casual conversation. Now,

I knew what an oncologist was and what kind of patients they treated. But believe it or not, I never connected her being an oncology fellow to Zackie's abdominal mass being cancerous.

That may sound crazy, but it's true. My only reason for sharing all those descriptive details is to prove how cognitively present I was while speaking with the doctor. Right at that very moment, I could've allowed the confirmation of the cancerous mass to crush me like a tin can, I could've allowed my emotions to put me in a state of shock and fear. I could've allowed myself to feel helpless. Believe me, the human part of me wanted to, but the spirit part of me, the place where God dwells, activated my force field of hope and faith and protected me from fear and doubt.

Don't ever disregard the way or how God comes to help you. For me, He blinded my mind from all the scary, bad and negative things I believed cancer to be. God covered me that Wednesday in October and protected my hope, until my strength to endure that Stage 4 Liver Cancer diagnosis caught up with my faith and trust in Him. When I came to myself, I grabbed hope by the hand and held on for dear life. It wasn't because I wasn't scared, because I was. I held on to hope, because I could feel the doubt, darkness and death begin to creep in. But I knew enough to keep confessing, "Zackie shall live and not die, this diagnosis is not unto death." Because of my belief and faith in Jesus Christ, I knew Zackie was already healed by His blood. I knew that, I believed that, and I confessed and stood on that. That's how I held on to hope—I believed, I trusted and had faith in what Jesus had already provided—healing. Remember, hope keeps you believing and believing keeps you in faith for a miracle. Don't ever let go of hope.

EXHAUSTED HOPE

Metastatic Hepatoblastoma. That's the medical name for the type of cancer Zackie had. This cancer was aggressive, fast-growing, and it began spreading quickly to his lungs. Zackie was in the fight of his young, precious life and he didn't even know it.

Chemotherapy treatments began immediately, which inevitably started the clock of time. My family and I didn't start the clock, the cancer did. In my opinion, chemotherapy is a necessary evil, if that makes any sense to you. I say this because chemo heals and chemo destroys you at the same time. I cannot tell you how helpless you feel as a mother, watching the chemo cycle begin along with the sickness that accompanies it, and a compromised immune system left to slowly rebuild itself.

There were days when my son's journey was so difficult and rough, I could feel the weight and the pressure of the ten-month process. My body began to manifest the stress and anxiety I was holding inside in the form of a rash. The Christmas Tree rash is what my doctor called it. The rash formed from one oval shaped bump on my back that spread into the pattern of Christmas tree

branches all over my torso, back and neck areas. Some days I felt so overwhelmed because decisions about surgery, days-long chemo, and transfusions had to be made without time to pray or think. All I could do was to have hope, faith and trust that God was with Zackie and would be a comfort to him during these hard days.

Those were the days I now call exhausted hope. Exhausted hope is when your hope weakens from hunger. Yes, hope needs to be fed. What do you feed hope to regain its strength? Faith of course, along with boldness, confidence, endurance and trust. Time will test and erode your hope when fatigue sets in. Be assured that you are in a battle and how you survive—the way your life turns out in the end depends on hope, faith, belief and trust.

These are the times when having a faith partner can be a source of strength for you. For me, it was my husband. We were going through this together, side by side. We were each other's faith partner through this experience, leaning on each other for support and strength. Working together to care for each other, our two sons, our church and our home. There isn't another person I'd rather go to war with than my husband; he is the strongest person I know. He was so encouraging and supportive and I'll never forget what he did for me the day Zackie passed away. He kept me distracted long enough for my faith and trust to regain enough strength to help plan our oldest son's birthday party and Zackie's Memorial Service.

Zackie passed away on August 2, 2014 at about 2:08 AM. By the time the sun came up, my husband had downloaded a gospel music CD for inspiration and made plans to take us to breakfast. At the time, I didn't want to do any of that, but my husband knew I needed it and I did. I felt encouraged and inspired to hold on to my hope, faith and trust in Jesus Christ.

Seth's birthday party was August 9, 2014 and Zackie's Memorial Service was August 16, 2014. We had a lot going on and I could not do any of it without my husband, my best friend. During those days, I drew strength from his strength and I still do today. And of course, God was always with me, providing strength and endurance along with His peace and comfort. Even as you read this book He is with you too, supplying you with strength, courage and determination to hope and to trust in Him.

RENEWED HOPE

Other days, I could feel my hope and faith in God stirring up on the inside of me, giving me the power to keep moving forward for Zackie. I kept hoping, I kept believing, and I kept my faith in God. God was right there with me through the absolute hardest time of my life. He provided peace when I was too anguished. He provided comfort when I felt tired. He provided calm when I was confused. He provided strength when I was weak. He provided joy when I was sad. And when I felt like I couldn't take another step, I could hear Him say "you can make it." Believe it or not, God did all of that for me through my son, Zackie. Going through this trauma, I'm sure, the worst days of his young life, he displayed peace when everything around him was so chaotic. Because his mom and dad were right there by his side, he was comforted. Even though he didn't like the white coats (the team of doctors), he was filled with joy and happiness. During this difficult time, Zackie became my hero because of his never quit, never give up attitude; it was absolutely remarkable to see.

There will be days when you feel like you can take on the world and win. You may also have days when you feel like you don't want to face the world. And it's ok. Both days are ok to experience, just don't let go of your hope. Hope is always your road map back to faith and believing. So, you may be down, but you're not out. You may be tired, but don't quit. You may be ready to give up, don't. Time has tested your faith, but you're still here. Don't let go of your hope. Remember, when this journey gets hard, hope, hope some more and continue to hope. Have faith and believe you will make it through and past this moment.

Use this time to recall the start of your experience until this very moment. Look for the God moments. They are the moments that when you think about them now, you realize God was working on your behalf. These moments are usually small and seemingly insignificant, but when remembered they carry a big feeling of gratefulness with them. God moments have the power to bring life to you in ways that no one but God can. These moments remind you that you are not in this alone. Though I experienced many God moments during this time, I'll share three of my greatest God moments with you.

HOPE IN GOD'S POWER

The most powerful and significant God moment I've ever experienced was during the transitioning of Zackie. As our son was literally breathing his last breaths of life, my husband asked me if I do hear music... I listened carefully, and I could. I could hear the most beautiful sound of music I've ever heard. It was the glorious sound of heaven's music. The music sounded like many voices of one sound in a continuous ascending pattern that was exalting and joyous in my best description. It was Jesus and the host of heaven coming to receive Zackie.

At the lowest, saddest time of our lives, God was with us. Never forsaking, never leaving us, just right there with us. My husband and I couldn't physically see anyone, but I'm certain the room was filled with the presence of heaven. To me, it was a miracle, a God moment that I have gratefully held in my heart. Our son's spirit was ushered into heaven on the worship of the heavenly host and received by Jesus—I will never forget that moment.

Another God moment happened the day after Zackie passed away. I remember my awesome husband being just that—awesome. Without using words, he kept me putting one foot in front of the other by occupying my mind and thoughts with faith and family. That night God gave me the most beautiful dream I've ever dreamt. It was of Zackie sitting in the most peaceful grassy field I've ever seen. He was sitting in the grass, legs folded Indian style with an incredibly peaceful smile of serenity upon his face.

When Zackie passed away, he was 21 months old, but in the dream he was about 4 years old. He was completely

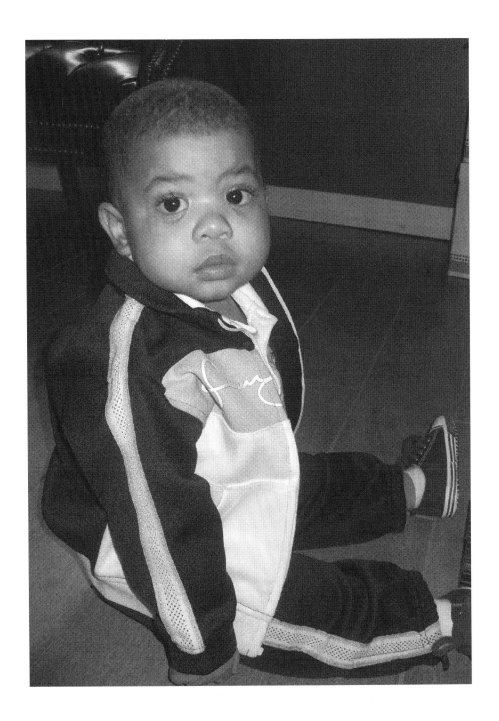

healed and made whole. He had a head full of curly hair, beautiful skin, and a strong body—none of which he had at his passing. I will never forget that smile upon his face, it was as if he was telling me, I'm ok, mom. I thank God for His love and comfort for me during that season of my life. I tell you; I have held on to that memory to this day. That dream, that God moment keeps me going, not grieving. It keeps me believing that one day I will be reunited with Zackie and what a day that will be.

My other God moment came shortly after the passing of Zackie. One Saturday morning I was lying in bed awake, but didn't have the energy or desire to get up. I just wanted to lie in bed and be sad. From another room, I could hear my husband and son talking. I remember thinking they were waiting on me to come out so we could get our day started. But I didn't want to get up, I just wanted to lie in bed and be sad. What happened next was my God moment.

Internally I could hear the voice of God say to me, "Get up, your family needs you." My spirit was shaken to its core as I received a boost of God's power. I attached my anchor of hope to God's love for me and jumped out of my bed so fast, full of hope in God's power to comfort and heal. God was there with me when I hit a low point, reviving and restoring His power that lives in me. Because He cares for and keeps me, I'm thankful to God that I've never had another day like that one.

I pray that my experience and stories have encouraged you to hope when all is lost, or when you don't know which way to turn. Remember to hope, it's the road map that leads to faith and believing. Never let go of hope, stay strong in faith and don't ever stop believing. God is always with you, walking beside you through the most difficult times in your life. Look for your God moments and recognize how He's working things out on your behalf.

Now we have this hope as a sure and steadfast anchor of the soul. It cannot slip, and it cannot break down under whoever steps out upon it—a hope that reaches farther and enters into the very certainty of the Presence within the veil. (Hebrews 6:19).

CHAPTER FIVE

FROM A BROTHER'S HEART

If I had to choose one word to describe our *Between the Treatments* time together as a family; it would be laughter. Zackie was only one when he got sick and he wasn't talking yet, but he used his face to tell us what he was thinking and feeling. We would laugh at the looks he gave us and how he used his hands and feet to join in the family fun. My little brother; he was so funny to me. It's still hard to believe Zackie's gone.

My name is Seth Sterling Antoine. I am thirteen years old now, but I was five years old when I got my little brother,

Zackie. I never asked mom and dad for a brother; I just didn't know I could do that. I secretly wished and even prayed for one, so I was very happy to finally get a little brother.

If anyone would ever ask me why I wanted a brother, my answer would be two reasons. In no particular order, my first reason was selfish. I wanted to be a big brother and have someone to play with. My second reason was selfless, believe it or not, I wanted to share my parents. I wanted someone else to experience the love my mom and dad showered me with. You see, my brother Zackie and I were adopted, and God loved us so much that He blessed us with the best mom and dad in the world. I wanted Zackie to experience the love, guidance and nurturing I had received for five years then, and still, to this very day I am loved by God and my parents. That's what I wanted for Zackie; that's why I wanted a brother.

We bonded instantly, even though Zackie was just a baby and couldn't talk or walk yet, I knew we would have a special brotherly bond. Days and weeks would pass, and I would run into his room to see if he had gotten big enough to play with... but not yet, he was still tiny and needed more time to grow. Zackie was worth waiting on because he was my brother and I loved him. So, while I waited on Zackie to grow, I would think about all the things I wanted to show him.

I wanted to show Zackie where his classroom would be at school, where the cafeteria was located and most importantly, where the boy's bathroom was so he could hide out when he needed a break from the class lesson. I wanted to show Zackie my acorn collection I had hidden in my yellow toolbox under my train table. The best of all, I wanted to show Zackie all of my trains. Oh yes, how can I forget about doggie? He was my favorite stuffed animal; I wanted to show Zackie that too. There were so many things I wanted to show him, so many things we didn't have time to get to. Our time as brothers lasted almost two years, not even

close to what Zackie and I wanted, which was forever. But, I thank a God for the time I had with Zackie and the fun memories we made as brothers. I believe God brought Zackie and I together, crossing our lives and paths together like David and Jonathan from the Bible.

When Zackie first went to the hospital, my mom and dad told me he wasn't feeling good. I didn't know why he was sick, but it made me sad to see my little brother lying there not feeling good. He didn't look or act like the Zackie I knew, full of energy and laughter. I would try to get into his hospital bed to make him feel better, like I had done many times at home. Like Zackie had done for me when I ran into a pole at school and had to go to the emergency room.

He laid next to me in my hospital bed laughing and smiling—I'm sure my head was still hurting, but Zackie made me feel better.

He was there for me when I was hurting, so I needed to be there for him while he was hurting. Other than getting into Zackie's hospital bed, another way I thought would help him feel better was my trains. He loved playing with my trains at home, so I would bring them when I visited him. The trains did help Zackie feel better, but they couldn't take his pain away. I was only six years old so I didn't know what cancer was and I really didn't know my brother could die from it.

I didn't like going to the hospital seeing my brother sick, but I did like all of the new things I could get into. The hospital had a huge play area outside and lots of kids to play with. It also had a playroom close to Zackie's room, so I would ask mom and dad to take me. When Zackie was feeling well, my parents would take him to the playroom too. There was one toy in the playroom that Zackie loved. It was the kind of toy babies would hold onto and push, I guess it helped them walk without falling. Well, it was Zackie's favorite and whenever he had to stay in the hospital, I hoped it was there because I knew it would make him happy. There was a window seat in Zackie's room that he enjoyed looking out of. We watched many soccer games from that window. He would play in that window for hours, rolling his favorite toy from one end to the other end of that window seat.

Whenever Zackie had to stay in the hospital our family had to separate. One of my parents stayed in the hospital with Zackie and I would go home with the other parent. I really didn't like that arrangement because it changed everything. I really wanted both of my parents to come home with me. I wanted all of us to be together like we used to be. That's why when Zackie was home from the hospital, family time was so important to us. Time at home, between Zackie's treatments was so much fun. We would play games, watch movies, play with our toys, and play in the bounce house in the yard.

They were the best times because we were all together. As much fun as we would have between Zackie's treatments, one time was really special to me. I was graduating from kindergarten and Zackie was still admitted in the hospital. My parents prayed and asked God to make a way for both of them to make it to my graduation. I wanted both of my parents there too. Zackie was discharged from the hospital and the whole family came to see me graduate. I was so happy and so was Zackie, because he couldn't keep still. He and dad had to watch the graduation from the back of the school's gym.

Sometime during the summer of 2014, Zackie's treatments were over. I was happy because he didn't have to stay in the hospital anymore. Zackie had always been special to me so I thought he was special to the hospital too because they sent a nurse to take care of Zackie at home. Just like I didn't know what cancer was, I didn't know a hospice nurse took care of someone until he passed away. I didn't understand that my brother was dying, I thought because he was home that he was ok. I was too young to process what I was seeing, but I'm glad my mom and dad brought Zackie home so we could spend time loving him.

When Zackie passed away, I didn't understand that either. I didn't understand where he went, because before I went to bed that night I saw my brother sleeping and then he was gone. My parents helped me understand where babies go when they pass away. They told me Zackie was in heaven with God and Jesus and that he was safe and healed. I know who God and Jesus are, so I know Zackie is ok.

Every time I think of my little brother it makes me sad. Sometimes I begin to cry because I miss him so much; I miss him a lot. My parents tell me that Zackie is in heaven right now and they share stories about the fun times we had, and they make me feel a little better. I know one day I will see Zackie again, but until then, I'll enjoy all of the memories I've shared with the best little brother anyone could ever ask for. I miss you Zackie.

MEMORIES

I have so many memories of Zackie, some I had forgotten until photographs and videos lovingly reminded me. Birthdays and holidays are a big deal in our family and my mom and dad can tell you, I especially love them too. I remember our first family holiday

with Zackie, Thanksgiving 2012. Zackie was still so tiny, he was only four weeks old. I remember sitting at the dinner table, daddy held Zackie while we ate, and I was so happy because of what was to happen after dinner. One of our family traditions is to decorate our Christmas tree after Thanksgiving dinner. I was so happy because I wanted to show Zackie the ornaments I made at school and the sparkly lights on the tree. I remember he sat in his baby seat, quietly observing us. At that moment, I wondered if he felt the love I wanted to share with him. I wondered if he would love Christmas as much as I do. I wondered so many things, but mostly about the fun times we would have as brothers.

Fun times like when Zackie was small, I would sneak into his room and climb into his crib. We used to play with my stuffed bear. I would pull the blanket over our heads and roar like a bear, so I called it bears. At first, Zackie didn't like that, but as time went on, he would look for me to climb into his crib to play with him. I would say, "Come on Zackie, it's time to play bears." What I didn't know was that mom and dad could hear that I was in Zackie's crib through the baby monitor; I was in so much trouble. Sometimes when I climbed into his crib we would just look around the room. He was so tiny that I had to be very careful not to hurt him. My parents would ask me not to wake him, but I wanted to play with my little brother.

When Zackie got older he looked forward to crawling into my room and playing with all of my toys. He would stand in his crib and wait on mom or dad to take him out so he could crawl into my room. Sometimes daddy would put Zackie into my bunk bed so we could play together; I always enjoyed that. Zackie would follow me around the room getting into everything and throwing my trains. I didn't like him throwing my trains, but I loved having him around.

Mom and dad would tell me how much Zackie missed me while I was at school. They would tell me how they tried to keep him out of my room, but he kept crawling in because he was looking for me. I would be so happy when the three o' clock school bell rang because that meant Zackie was waiting for me in the car. I had missed him all day and couldn't wait to see him. We would laugh and talk all the way home; it was like we had our own language because we understood each other.

My parents would give me time to relax before starting my homework, so I spent it with Zackie. Our favorite thing to do after school was to watch the Chica Show, it was Zackie's favorite show. He sat on the ottoman in his baby seat and I sat in front of the ottoman on the floor.

Nothing made me more happy, except when Zackie would put his feet on my head, that was my favorite thing.

Seth & Zack. I always did and still do love the sound of Seth & Zack. By the way, I pray that prayer every day and still include Zackie in my prayers because he was so special to me. I'm so grateful that mom, dad and I had the *chance* to love and take care of him. I'm so grateful for the *chance* to be his big brother. I'm so grateful for the memories we made. As much as I love and miss Zackie, I know he's in heaven with God and Jesus and he's not sick anymore. He will always be my little brother and best friend.

Father,

thank You for this day,

thank You for daddy, mama, Seth and Zack.

In Jesus' Name I pray, Amen.

– Seth Antoine

CHAPTER 6

GOOD COUNTS

Good counts is a term used by doctors and nurses when your blood work is in an appropriate range for discharge from the hospital. Whenever Zackie's chemo cycle was complete, his immune system was beat up pretty badly. It had to slowly get strong enough to fight off infections and other compromising attacks, which is code for long hospital stays.

The nurses would draw blood several times a day to check the numbers of his blood. When Zackie's results were too low, the doctors and nurses would say his counts are not good enough for discharge. There were times when his immune system was so compromised, he needed platelets and blood transfusions to help in the recovery process. When Zackie's results were at safe levels, the doctors and nurses would say his counts are good and he's ready to be discharged.

During those ten months, so much emphasis was placed on good COUNTS, understandably so. But now we want to place the emphasis on GOOD counts. What's the difference, you ask? I'm happy to tell you.

Zackie was twenty one months old when he passed away. At the time of this writing, he's been gone six years, way longer than he was alive. Please trust me when I tell you that Zackie was a gift and an assignment from God. Our job was to love, nurture, take care of and walk beside him during a grueling ten-month fight with cancer. Zackie brought a lot of love, joy and affection into our family. So, we want to focus on the GOOD he brought and shared with us in the little time we had with him.

These are just a few GOOD counts memories of Zackie. The love and laughter that he brought to our family and our hearts were byproducts of his big personality. These are true stories, so I hope you find them as funny as we did and still do.

TROUBLE IN THE HOUSE

Playing board games is one of our family's favorite pass times. Our favorite game to play is Trouble. We would gather around the game—my husband, Seth, Zackie and me. My husband always played with the red cones, he said, "Red is for the Blood of Jesus." Seth always played with the yellow cones. I played with the blue cones and Zackie just watched until one day he decided he wanted to play too.

Out of the blue, he placed his tiny hand on the pop-o-matic bubble, pressed as hard as he could and moved the closest cone to him. My husband, Seth and I burst into laughter, we were not expecting that. He must have watched us pop and move, pop and move a thousand times. So he said to himself, "I can do that, I can pop and move too." And he did, although he only touched the bubble once, he played Trouble with his family. I don't remember whose cone he moved or who won the game, but clearly Zackie was the champion that day because of the lasting memory he created. From that day to this one we still talk about how funny that moment was.

I'M COMING DADDY

Zackie had a way of inviting himself to be a part of everything others were doing. It was his way of accomplishing his two favorite things—playing and being near his family. Well, it was no different when daddy was ready to play his golf game. Scene: Daddy grabbed the iPad, sat on the sofa, started the app, the music started playing and here comes Zackie. Every time he heard the music he stopped whatever he was doing because he knew daddy was playing golf and he wanted to play too.

Zackie would push and wiggle his little body into daddy's lap. He would start playing by using his tiny hands

to tap any part of the screen he could reach. When daddy would move the screen out of his reach, Zackie would stretch out his short legs to use his feet to tap the screen. When the game was over he had this way of looking at daddy as to say you're welcome, or aren't you glad I helped you? Needless to say, daddy ended up with a very high score which isn't very good in golf. When they were finished playing, daddy's ranking was destroyed, but he was happy because Zackie helped him swing, chip and putt.

I CAN HELP YOU WITH THAT

Zackie was a very, very, very picky eater. Believe it or not, other than baby formula the only foods he ever ate were green beans and pears baby food, which makes this GOOD count story very funny.

Whenever we ate dinner or anything really, Zackie would pick something off of my plate and put it in my mouth for me. It didn't matter what I was eating, he thought it was very important to feed me. Now, he would never attempt to sneak or eat any of my food—so weird right—he just wanted to feed me.

I vividly remember one day we were waiting in a hospital exam room; Zackie was sitting on my lap with his back to me. I began to eat a bag of chips, and wouldn't

you know it Zackie stuck his tiny hand in the bag, pulled out a chip, turned his hand backwards and put it in my mouth. My husband and I looked at each other and burst into laughter. This is one of my favorite memories of Zackie because he was so sick at that time, but his beautiful personality always shined through.

I THINK I'LL JUST KICK MY FEET UP

Zackie loved his family. My husband and I felt his love every moment of every day, but the one person he loved the most was his big brother, Seth. Zackie absolutely loved playing with his brother. On the weekends, Seth would wake up early and crawl into Zackie's crib and they'd play what Seth called "bears." On weekday mornings, we would take Zackie out of his crib and he would crawl right into Seth's room to get a little more play time in before Seth went off to

school. Except Zackie didn't know where Seth disappeared to for hours and hours every day.

So throughout the day, Zackie would crawl into Seth's room looking for him, playing with his toys, and hoping to see him soon. When Seth returned home from school, Zackie would be so happy to see him. Seth, of course tired from a long school day would just lay across the ottoman. And Zackie, in true little brother fashion, would put his feet on Seth's head and cross his ankles as to say, I've been waiting for you all day and you're not getting away. Zackie did this every day. Seth would come home, lay on the ottoman, and Zackie would use Seth's head as his ottoman. He would patiently wait for Seth to get up so the playing, laughing and chasing could start.

WASH ME AND LEAVE ME... ALONE

Ahhhh! Taking a bath was very enjoyable for Zackie, in fact he loved it! He loved the warm water on his skin. He loved the little bubbles the soap made. He loved the gentle head scratch as his hair was being shampooed. He loved playing in the water. He loved being dried off and wrapped in a towel.

Errrrrrr! No really, this is really the end of this story. After his bath was over, the enjoyment came to a screeching halt. Everything that came after being wrapped in the towel requires audio because I don't know how to spell the screams he made when it was time to be lotioned and dressed.

If Dr Seuss made Zackie's screams into a book, it would read like this.

BABY LOTION AND CLOTHES

By: Zackie (To the tune of Green Eggs and Ham)

I don't like to be lotioned in the morning,

I don't like to be lotioned at night,

I don't like to be lotioned mom, alright?

Don't dress me on the bed,

Don't dress me on the floor,

Come on mom, what are clothes even for?

I think you get the picture by now. This happened every time he took a bath.

I hope you have enjoyed the *GOOD* counts stories of our bossy, opinionated, but loving son. Yes, it's been hard not having Zackie here with us, but we are alright because we know exactly where he is. He's in heaven—with God and Jesus—awaiting our arrival. My husband and I often talk about going to heaven and after meeting God and Jesus (WOW!), the very next person we want to see is Zackie. Our life together as a family is different without him, but these stories and many, many more are what we think of when we think of Zackie. We focus on the GOOD he brought into our family and the GOOD his foundation is doing to help others. Along with our hope, faith and trust that we will see Zackie again, the loving memories of him bring the laughter and that is the medicine for our souls.

You or someone you love dearly, as was the case for us, may be having a difficult time right now. But when, not if you remember the GOOD counts and the God moments, you will smile and laugh too. Even if it's for a few moments, you will have managed to focus on someone or something else instead of your hurt and pain. Yes, your pain is real, but it's not permanent. So, let your loving memories become the medicine for your soul. Remain hopeful even in the darkest of times, because hope always finds a way to let the light shine through.

CHAPTER SEVEN

GOVERNED BY GRACE

As previously mentioned in chapter one, I want to talk about what grace is. Grace is not a denomination or movement, grace is a person, and that person is my Lord and Savior Jesus Christ. In this chapter titled *Governed by Grace*, I want to begin by sharing with you how at one of the worst times of our life, our belief in Jesus Christ got us through.

A STORY FROM THE PAST

Let me start by telling you a story about myself from years ago when I worked at 84 Lumber. In 1988 or 1989 I began to work at 84 Lumber. I drove the truck and made deliveries to builders. I delivered lumber, sheet rock, and housing supplies. It was then I discovered something called a governor. This was something that 84 Lumber put on the truck to keep us from going too fast. Let me explain by giving you the definition of a governor; Governor: a device for maintaining uniform speed regardless of changes of load, as by regulating the supply of fuel or working fluid.

To our amazement, this device was placed on the truck by the management staff. No matter how much I pushed down on the gas or what I did, that truck would only go so fast. It actually frustrated me to no extent. I was a young guy used to going fast, I liked to get where I'm going without wasting time and now I was being governed by the small device placed on the truck by the company to keep their drivers from speeding. Can you imagine being in your 20s or 30s smashing down on the gas thinking that you're about to get there with this load, and you're ready to go to your destination, and all of a sudden the truck has been wired to only go a certain speed.

Look at the definition of the word governor again, a device for maintaining uniform speed regardless of change of load, as by regulating the supply of fuel or working fluid. Wow! They placed that little device on the truck to actually save on gas, and to protect their equipment. I thought it was only there to keep me from going too fast, but instead, it was for my protection also.

Let me tell you about my God's grace. Just like that job wanted to protect their investment and employee, God also wants to help protect you from harm. He has given us a Lord and Savior named Jesus Christ. You see, grace is not a denomination or a movement, it is a person and His name is Jesus.

Let's look at a story in the Bible about a man named Paul who had an issue and sought the Lord for help.

"It is not expedient for me doubtless to glory. I will come to visions and revelations of the Lord. I knew a man in Christ above fourteen years ago, (whether in the body, I cannot tell; or whether out of the body, I cannot tell: God knoweth;) such an one caught up to the third heaven. And I knew such a man, (whether in the body, or out of the body, I cannot tell: God knoweth;) How that he was caught up into paradise, and heard unspeakable words, which it is not lawful for a man to utter. Of such an one will I glory: yet of myself I will not glory, but in mine infirmities. For though I would desire to glory, I shall not be a fool; for I will say the truth: but *now* I forbear, lest any man should think of me above that which he seeth me *to be,* or *that* he heareth of me. And lest I should be exalted above measure through the abundance of the revelations, there was given to me a thorn in the flesh, the messenger of Satan to buffet me, lest I should be exalted above measure. For this thing I besought the Lord thrice, that it might depart from me. And he said unto me, **My grace is sufficient for thee: for my strength is made perfect in weakness.** Most gladly therefore will I rather glory in my infirmities, that the power of Christ may rest upon me. Therefore I take pleasure in infirmities, in reproaches, in necessities, in persecutions, in distresses for Christ's sake: for when I am weak, then am I strong"

(II Corinthians 12:1-10 [Amplified Bible]).

As you can tell in these Scriptures, Paul is explaining that he had a vision or a dream that he was taken into the third heaven. He talks about an experience that he had when he got to heaven.

The experience was so overwhelming that he was reluctant to talk about everything he saw. When the dream/vision was over, he was given a thorn in his flesh to keep him humble. The thorn is a spirit that would vex him continually. God allowed the spirit to mess with Paul because He knew His grace was sufficient.

Notice in the story that Paul asked God several times to deliver him from this thorn to no avail. God told him that His grace was sufficient for him. I want you to pay close attention to God's response to Paul. He says that His grace is sufficient. I'm not saying that what you are going through in your life is caused by God. I'm simply saying that God is always there to help you through any and everything you're going through. Whenever we face trials and tribulations in life, we must always remember, He is a very present help in times of need.

THE ROMAN CENTURION

The way you see Jesus, the revelation that you have of Him, will not affect God's acceptance of you. But it will affect your acceptance of what God has for you. It will affect how you receive from Him.

Consider the Roman centurion who told Jesus, "You don't have to come to my house. Just speak the word and my servant at home will be healed" (Luke 7:6-7).

Compare him with Jairus, the ruler of a synagogue, who told Jesus, "My daughter is dying. Please come to my house and lay Your hands on her, and she shall live" (Mark 5:22-23).

Do you know that Jesus does not have to go to your house to heal you? So why did Jesus follow Jairus to his house? Jesus had to come down to Jairus's level of faith. Jairus believed that his daughter could be healed, but only if Jesus came and laid His hands on her. Remember, it's according to your faith. It's going to work for you according to how you believe.

The centurion was different. He said, "Lord, You don't have to come to my house. I know who You are."

This centurion believed that Jesus did not have to come to his house for his servant to be healed. He believed that Jesus only needed to speak the word. He said to Jesus, "Just speak the word and my servant at home will be healed."

Do you know who Jesus is? The centurion had a greater understanding of who Jesus is than Jairus, the ruler of the synagogue, and he wasn't even a Jew!

Jesus asked His disciples, "Why are you so fearful? How is it that you have no faith?" (Mark 4:40). He even remarked, "O you of little faith." (Matthew 6:30). But to the woman whose daughter was demon-possessed, He said, "O woman, great is your faith!" (Matthew 15:28). And to the centurion, He declared, "I have not found such great faith, not even in Israel!"

My desire is for you to have an accurate understanding of who Jesus is because when your revelation of Jesus is big, you will know what has been freely given to you.

And when you know what is yours in Christ Jesus, you will be rich in all things!

I know it seems like nothing can comfort you right now, and even the thought of someone saying they understand your pain makes you angry. It is in these moments of life that we tend to be mad with the world. There is a grace that can help, and His name is Jesus. He is always right there ready to assist you in times of trouble. Let me give you a few scriptures that can help. I pray these scriptures can comfort you, as it did us, as we tried to navigate life between the treatments.

"For the law was given by Moses, *but* grace and truth came by Jesus Christ."

(John 1:17 [Amplified Bible)]).

"For if because of one man's trespass (lapse, offense) death reigned through that one, much more surely will those who receive [*God's*] overflowing grace (unmerited favor) and the free gift of righteousness [*putting them into right stand-ing with Himself*] reign as kings in life through the one Man Jesus Christ (the Messiah, the Anointed One)"

(Romans 5:17 [Amplified Bible)]).

"I have told you these things, so that in Me you may have [*perfect*] peace and confidence. In the world you have tribulation and trials and distress and frustration; but be of good cheer [*take courage; be confident, certain, undaunt-ed*]! For I have overcome the world. [*I have deprived it of power to harm you and have conquered it for you.*]"

(John 16:33 [Amplified Bible)]).

GRACED TO REST IN THE LORD

"THEREFORE, WHILE the promise of entering His rest still holds and is offered [*today*], let us be afraid [*to distrust it*], lest any of you should think he has come too late and has come short of [*reaching*] it. For indeed we have had the glad tidings [*Gospel of God*] proclaimed to us just as truly as they [*the Israelites of old did when the good news of deliverance from bondage came to them*]; but the message they heard did not benefit them, because it was not mixed with faith (with the leaning of the entire personality on God in absolute trust and confidence in His power, wisdom, and goodness) by those who heard it; neither were they united in faith with the ones [*Joshua and Caleb*] who heard (did believe). For we who have believed (adhered to and trusted in and relied on God) do enter that rest, in accordance with His declaration that those [*who did not believe*] should not enter when He said, As I swore in My wrath, They shall not enter My rest; and this He said although [*His*] works had been completed and prepared [*and waiting for all who would believe*] from the foundation of the world.

For in a certain place He has said this about the seventh day: And God rested on the seventh day from all His works. And [*they forfeited their part in it, for*] in this [*passage*] He said, They shall not enter My rest. Seeing then that the promise remains over [*from past times*] for some to enter that rest, and that those who formerly were given the good news about it and the opportunity, failed to appropriate it and did not enter because of disobedience"

(Hebrews 4:1-6 [Amplified Bible]).

Rest means a causing to cease or refreshment. The grace of God is readily available to help us find rest in moments of difficulties. I want you to notice what it says in Hebrews chapter 4: "There is still a rest that remain for the children of God."

I want you to clearly understand what I am saying right now. Grace has been given to us through Jesus

Christ. The Bible says in John chapter 1 and verse 17, that the law was given to Moses but grace and truth came by Jesus Christ.

So we understand that Jesus is grace, and the grace I'm talking to you about is our Lord and Savior Jesus Christ.

At one of the worst times of our lives, my family and I could not turn to family members. We could not turn to friends. We could not even turn to our church family. All of whom we knew loved us, but we needed something greater than what any human being could offer.

I remember talking to people who responded to me with, "I just didn't know what to say. I didn't call you because I just didn't know what to say." We heard that repeatedly, over and over and over again. At first you find yourself getting upset.

You get mad and angry because you hoped that some of the people that you have been there for, people you have done things for would understand what you're going through. The surprise was they just didn't understand. Sometimes we just don't have adequate words to help someone in need when they're between treatments.

Remember, this chapter is titled *Governed by Grace*, and what I'm offering you is what allowed my family and I to make it through one of the worst seasons of our lives—and that was the great grace that governed our lives. It kept us from being too high or too low, from not wanting to get out of the bed, or wanting to throw the covers over our heads. God's grace kept us through it all.

Grace is someone and His name is Jesus. He actually knows every single thing you're going through.

The Bible says in Hebrews chapter 4:16-18: "We have a high priest that is well acquainted with everything we would ever go through. When we find ourselves in times of need, we can boldly come to the throne of God and receive grace and mercy to help us. He is a very present help in times of need, just when we need it."

Listen beloved! At the worst time of your life Jesus is right there with open arms. He's willing to hold you, willing to dry the tears from your eyes, willing to carry the heavy load and burdens.

God is not angry with you. I don't know what you're facing. I don't know what you're dealing with, but one thing that I can say, please don't blame yourself. It is not your fault.

God is readily available 24/7, 365 days a year. You can go to God and find grace and mercy to help. He is a very present help in the time of need.

I really want you to understand that God is not mad with you. God is not angry with you. God is not the cause of what you're dealing with. I hear you, I hear what you're saying, I hear your thoughts. If God is not angry with me, and if God is not after me, if God is not punishing me, then please tell me why am I going through all of this pain?

We live in a fallen world and things happen. We live in a world that is broken and getting worse and worse, so we have to learn how to navigate through the various issues that arise in our lives.

You can go to the throne of a loving, kind, and gentle Father who will wrap His arms around you, and wipe the tears from your eyes. He will do everything He can to assure you that He loves you and He is with you. He is for you. That's why He sent His only begotten Son into the world to help save you and to give you eternal life.

The Bible says in Romans 8:1: "Therefore, there is now no condemnation to them that walk after the spirit. Our God is a loving Father, who cares deeply for us. He will never do anything to you to destroy your life. He's right there with you between every situation you find yourself in. Now it's time to learn how to rest in the Lord."

HOW TO REST

Let me explain to you how you can actually find rest even at the worst point of your life. I hear you saying, how do you expect me to rest at the worst time of my life? Don't you know my baby is in the hospital? Don't you know my wife has been diagnosed with cancer?

Don't you know that the doctor just gave me the worst report I've ever heard of? The bank is talking about re-possessing my car. My house is being foreclosed. My child is failing in school. My job is downsizing and laying me off, and you're telling me that I can find rest? What possible rest can I find at the worst season of my life? It is at these moments of difficulties that we find ourselves in that the rest that God offers, is a mental rest that causes the rest of our body to function properly. The mental rest when you're not up all night struggling and straining, thinking about how you can handle this, how are you going to deal with this, how can you make it through what you're going through.

First Peter 5:7 says: "Cast all of your cares on the Lord, for He cares for you."

CASTING TIME

I want you to picture a container. I want you to put everything in your mind in that container. I want you to write each one of your issues down on a paper. I want you to write sickness, home foreclosure, car repossession, bad doctor's diagnosis, job downsizing, divorce papers, on and on and on, etc., etc., etc. I want you to write that down and put it in the container. I want you to take a chair and place that chair in the center of your room. I want you to do this for me.

I'm right there with you. You can do it. I want you to visualize that God is sitting in that chair. I want you to walk over to that chair as you visualize God sitting in the chair. Don't be fearful. God is not going to be angry with you. He's not going to strike you down. He's not going to curse you. I want you to take that container and dump it at the foot of that chair. I want you to picture that you are literally casting all of your cares at the feet of God. I want you to walk away.

This is how you cast your cares on Him. By simply dumping it at His feet. You see, the only way we will literally find rest is that we must dump out of our minds all of the things that bring us anguish, anxiety, pain, and trouble.

We must dump these issues out of our hearts. It may seem difficult, but if you're truly going to find rest, if you're truly going to find a place of rest in your mind, you are going to have to dump what's causing you to feel that way. God offers us an opportunity to come to Him and to cast our cares on Him.

I want you to take a deep breath and just trust me for a moment. Repeat this statement, "I don't care." Say it again, "I don't care."

I'm not asking you not to care in the sense that you're not going to do what you need to do. I am asking you not to carry the weight of that care in your mind on a daily basis.

Let Him carry the weight of it. Let Him deal with it while you are being led by Him to do what you need to do without the weight of the trouble that's causing you the pain and the grief.

Remember the Bible tells us to cast our cares on Him for He cares about us. I have repeatedly said God is not mad with you. God is not after you. God is not trying to hurt you. He is not the reason for your pain. He is not judging you. He is not trying to hurt you. God is not trying to teach you some lesson by causing you to go through the pain that you're going through. I want you to really think about this. If you have children of your own and you love those children, you would do anything for them. There is nothing you would not do or give up for your kids to have advantages in life. True or false?

Why do you allow your mind to even begin to wrap itself around the thought that a loving God like we have would teach you a lesson by bringing you through pain and anguish in the worst season of your life? The Bible tells us that if we know how to give our children good gifts, how much more does our heavenly Father desires to give us good gifts. The Bible says in the book of James that every good and perfect gift comes from God. It doesn't say every pain and hurt comes from God. I believe that God has taken a bad rap—that people are blaming every hurricane, tornado, car accident, plane crash, helicopter crash, and every tragedy on God. We live in a fallen world and things happen. God is the One that stands readily available to assist, heal, and love you. He wants to wrap His arms around you because He cares deeply about you. If you really want to know if somebody loves you, judge them by their actions.

God counts the hairs on your head, because He loves you just that much. The Bible says every time you cry He puts your tears in a bottle. Every tear that falls out of your eyes, He catches it and puts it in a bottle. Every time you pray to Him, He puts it in a bowl. He puts your prayers in a bowl, your tears in a bottle, and He knows how many hairs are on your head.

God is not like the people who disappointed you. You cannot judge a heavenly, spiritual Father on how you've been treated by earthly human beings. I'm sorry that maybe it was your father or mother that walked out and never came back, but God is not like that. The Bible says that God is not a man that He should lie. Neither is He the Son of Man that He should repent. If He said it, it must come to pass.

The Bible says in the book of Isaiah 55 verse 10 and 11: "Every word that proceeded out of God's mouth He sits over His word to make sure it accomplishes what He sent it to accomplish. It will not come back to Him void."

I'm talking about a God that cannot lie. A God that has never lied. God has done everything He has ever said He would do. I'm telling you to trust God. When He tells you to cast your cares on Him, it is because He is ready to help walk you through the worst season of your life. He is not the cause of the season you're going through. He can be the answer you need.

RECEIVING REST

Let me explain to you the way to receive His rest. The Bible says in Hebrews chapter 4 that God intended to give the people of Israel a true rest, but because of unbelief, and refusing to accept His way of rest, they did not receive the rest they were looking for. God sent His only Son Jesus Christ to the world to die for our sins. It was God's plan from the beginning of the world to restore man back to Himself. His plan included giving us the rest we needed from toiling, laboring, and trying to fix our lives on our own. He chose the people of Israel to show the world who He really is. It is through the finished work of Jesus Christ on the cross that affords you the opportunity to believe in that finished work and receive all that He has in store for you.

There is a rest that remain if you would just simply believe. I know it's been difficult because you're trying to fix this all by yourself. You're stressed, your body is filled with anxiety, and you're trying to figure it out on your own. Regardless to what the problem is—if you're in the hospital trying to deal with the doctors, the nurses, if the bill collectors are calling, if your spouse is talking about divorcing, if your children just told you that they hate you and they want to run away from home, if the job is talking about laying you off or perhaps downsizing—no matter what issues you are facing—believe me when I say that God is not in some distant place watching all of this happening. He is right there beside you with His arms stretched out saying, my son, my daughter, I want to give you rest. Remember I told you to picture God sitting in a chair? It's because He wants to bear all of your burdens.

He wants to carry the load of your problems. I want you to bring all of your problems and cast them on Him because He cares for you. This is how you receive His rest, by simply believing and receiving it.

Again, God is not the cause of these problems. He is a loving Father and He stands readily available to help you with every situation in your life.

AN OLD PROVERB

There's a story of a man walking along the beach and he noticed that there were two sets of footprints in the sand. As long as the sun was shining, and the day was beautiful, and the sea was calm, he noticed the two sets of footprints.

But when the clouds blocked the sun, when the winds began to blow, and the storms began to rise, he noticed only one set of footprints. He said, "Lord, as long as there were no problems I noticed two sets of footprints. Why is it that when things got bad I noticed only one set of footprints? Why did You leave me? Why did You forsake me?" It was then that God alerted him, "My son, my child, that one set of footprints was Mine." At the worst season of your life, it was then that I began to carry you.

You see beloved, the world would have you to believe that God runs away when times get hard. He is right there ready to carry you. He is ready to carry your worries, problems, anxiety, your stress—longing to relieve you from all that harm and hurt you.

I hear you. I hear you asking the question. I want to believe you. I want to believe what you're saying but why is it that He doesn't just take it away? Let me explain why that is.

RECEIVING HIS HELP

God made us a free moral agent. He created a world and then He gave that world to us. He runs the heavens, but He has given the earth to the children of men. God is a loving Father that is always raising us, training us, and teaching us through His love. He will never take back from us the freedoms that He has given us.

We often brag about this is our world, and we're going to do what we want. We're excited about the freedoms that we enjoy except when things don't go right. God wants us to master our lives, to run our lives, and yes, even to run this world He created. He cannot get involved in any of our situations without our permission. Just like we saw in Hebrews chapter 4. There is a rest that remains to them that receives it by faith. That's how you receive His rest. You believe with your heart and you tell Him, Father, I need You now! I want you to confess this with me:

"Father, I can't carry this alone. I cannot deal with these problems by myself. I need Your help. I need You to help me with this. I surrender to Your will and Your ways."

I want you to picture yourself giving Him all of your problems and casting them at His feet. I want you to leave them there. Let Him deal with the weight of it.

Now, since the pressure of the weight and problems are lifting off of you, no longer will you rehearse the problems over and over in your head, trying to figure out how you're going to deal with them. You have given it to Him. He has already fixed it. I want you to rest. Rest doesn't mean there is nothing else you need to do; it simply means a mental rest from worrying and anxiety. It is an acceptance that you're not alone. You have someone here ready to help you, and ready to help you carry this burden all the way to the finish line.

It is my heart's desire that you have received the rest you need to deal with these problems. I hope that this chapter on the grace of God has been inspirational to you. As you deal with your new normal of life between the treatments or perhaps some other issues, you have found a grace that is readily available to assist you.

We have found that the grace of God has helped us through one of the toughest seasons of our life. If it had not been for our Lord and Savior, we wouldn't have been able to make it, or write this book.

Father, we thank You for giving our readers the strength they need to make it through these difficult times in their lives. We praise You for always being a very present help in times of trouble. We ask You to allow our readers to sense Your presence in their lives. Let them know that You are right there with them. We thank You now! In Jesus Name, Amen!!

CHAPTER EIGHT

THE LAST DAYS

THE LAST DAYS – THROUGH A MOTHER'S EYES

It is said, in order to find out the end of something, start at the beginning. For us, the end began with the decision.

THE DECISION

I can remember exactly where we were when the decision was made. We were in the car, driving through one of our city's busiest intersections. We were discussing our options; should we keep going with chemo or should we stop? Those were our two options. Zackie had already received several rounds of chemo, but it wasn't working. The cancer was still spreading, and he couldn't receive a liver transplant. So, we made the hardest decision we would ever have to make. We decided when Zackie's chemo cycle was over and if the CAT scan still showed the cancer was spreading, we would not continue with any more chemotherapy combinations or treatments.

There, we said it. That was it. We decided not to put Zackie through anymore poking and prodding and experimenting. It was very hard to say and do because it felt like we were giving up, but it was the right decision for Zackie because he was so miserable. His childhood had been replaced with pain instead of playing, with fighting instead of fun. Other than wondering, I don't even know how the tumor or chemo made him feel because he was too young to tell me. Even now, I still can't find the words to express how helpless I felt. I would have done anything to take Zackie's pain away or to make his tummy stop swelling. I just wanted to see the tumor that was hurting my son because I wanted to kill *it*.

"Didn't you know? I mean you had to have known, right? When Zachary's stomach got big, didn't you know something was wrong?" When we told the doctors we decided to stop the chemotherapy treatments, those were the questions one of the doctors on Zackie's team asked us just before recommending hospice care for Zackie's final days. As if to imply that we, on purpose, waited until our son's cancerous liver tumor that we didn't know he had, would grow and advance to stage four before we would bring him to the doctor. I don't know if you or someone you love dearly has ever been asked those questions. But let me just say it took every ounce of everything godly within us not to respond in the tone of how the questions were asked. So, we politely asked the doctor, would you, on purpose, wait until your child's cancerous liver tumor grew and advanced to stage four before you brought him to the doctor? The doctor just looked at us with a look of conviction and we said neither would we.

When the care shifts from chemotherapy to hospice, things change and get weird. Suddenly, people in the hospital that we've talked with and visited with for months began to avoid us. People started talking to us as if Zackie had already passed away. So, when we were given the option of allowing Zackie to remain in the hospital or take him home during his hospice care, we took him home. Ohhhh! Zackie loved to be at home, where everyone and everything was familiar... *Between the Treatments* time again. Only, there weren't any more treatments to come. No more chemotherapy and no more hospital stays. All we had was faith, trust in God and expectation for a miracle for Zackie. Our faith in God was strong, so we kept our eyes on Him and trusted that He would never leave us.

HEARTBREAK AND HOPE

Deciding on which hospice company to choose is very much like choosing a funeral home to plan a funeral while you're still alive. While we all should plan our funeral before death so others can know what we want said and done, it's undesirable, so we don't touch it with a ten-foot pole. So, like most people we didn't want to have anything to do with hospice, but we had to choose one because Zackie needed care.

When calls from the hospice company began, it felt like a wave crashing over us. It felt like they were coming in to wait for Zackie's body to die while we were waiting for the miracle in his body. So, we planted our faith deep in Christ Jesus, our solid rock, because this wave was trying to move our footing. We had to keep our faith and trust in God because the hospice company didn't believe like we believed. We had to guard our hearts and spirits against fear and doubt because the hospice company wasn't in agreement with us for Zackie's miracle. They were coming in to facilitate death while we were fighting death with our faith.

I remember the first day someone from the hospice company came to our home, it was June 25, 2014. The hospice company needed to come over to have papers signed, so we let Seth and Zackie play in the yard until our meeting time. Seth was running around in the grass, laughing and playing.

Zackie was sitting in his toy car just looking around; he was squinting his eyes because it was sunny and hot. He was wearing a blue baseball cap to block the sun while he sat in his red car holding on to the black

steering wheel. Zackie had this thing about grass—he didn't like it at all. We tried again, as we would often do, to get him to stand in the grass, but he was not having it. So, we just laughed, talked, took pictures and videos and enjoyed our time together as a family. That was the last day Zackie was outside just being a child. Not on the way to a chemo treatment or being rushed to the emergency room because of excruciating pain. Not on the way to have a CAT scan or blood transfusion. He wasn't connected to an IV pole or feeding machine. He was free— for those moments while we were waiting—he was free to be a twenty-month-old child.

As the representative from the hospice company spoke, phrases like unnecessary measures and expected death were used throughout the conversation. He explained how if Zackie's health worsened, no extraordinary measures would be taken to save his life. He also explained how when a death is expected, the family is given expected death documents to keep in the home and the vehicle's glove box. I remember thinking and asking how can extraordinary measures be unnecessary for a baby, a child, a precious, innocent baby? My baby, my child, my precious, innocent baby. How could resuscitation for my son be considered unnecessary, but in hospice it was. If you or anyone you love were ever given an expected death document, I'm sorry you had to experience the pain associated with that. Others have no idea how much weight one sheet of paper weighs.

When Zackie's hospice care began, he was very sick and in a lot of pain. The hospice company thought Zackie had about a week left to live, so they only approved enough supplies and in home care for a week. But, in the true spirit of a faith fight, which we were clearly in, Zackie lived past their expectations. The house quickly filled up with oxygen machines, IV poles, and bags of medical supplies. Zackie's hospice care began, but our hearts and spirits remained hopeful. The hospice nurse that was assigned to Zackie was amazed by how long he was holding on. She was nice and very knowledgeable about the care she was providing. To distract Zackie from her care routine, she would tell stories and show videos of her chickens. Seth really enjoyed her chicken stories and videos; he would laugh and ask questions. Zackie would listen with his ears, but he always kept his eyes on her.

From the beginning of Zackie's care, the nurse showed us areas on his body that were already dying and what to be on the lookout for. It was very hard to hear and see what she was saying, but we were still hopeful and standing in faith, believing in God for Zackie's miracle. My heart was breaking for my son, he was hurting, dying before my eyes, but my hope was anchored in Christ Jesus. He was the only One who could heal or save Zackie. He was the only One who could heal my broken heart and cure the pain I was feeling, so I kept my hope and trust in Him. Admittedly, my faith was not perfect, there were days when I felt crushed by the weight of it all, exhausted and fatigued, but I never let go of my hope. It's what kept me being able to cry out, "God please help me."

FAITH AND FIGHTING

Days and weeks passed and Zackie was still fighting to live. Morphine was controlling the pain, but there were days when the pain would overtake the morphine. I remember days when we had to wait for the morphine to catch up to Zackie's pain. When the pain was too much to bear, as it often was, the nurse instructed us to use the bolas button. There was a button, in addition to the intravenous morphine, to press for a bolus shot and it would dispense extra morphine to help with the pain.

The bolas button was on a timer and it wouldn't dispense more morphine before the allotted time and dose. So, we would sit and wait for time to pass to give Zackie another bolus shot. There were times when it would take three to four bolus shots before he would settle down from the pain. To this day I am still amazed by how much pain he was in, yet he never complained. He just looked to mom, dad, and brother for his comfort. So, we showered him with love, attention and affection and for him that was all he needed. Yes, the morphine was for his body, but the love we gave him was for his soul.

During those days, Zackie began to sleep more and more and longer and longer. He stopped eating physically and his body began to reject the tube feeding. His body was starving, but because it was also dying, Zackie couldn't feel the hunger.

The weight loss was unbearable to watch; he was a shell of himself—the healthy, playful baby he was ten months earlier. Then it happened, he began to slowly disconnect from this world and his reality for the supernatural encounters he began to experience. Those days were excruciatingly hard to watch.

It was obvious and evident that Zackie was experiencing something supernatural. He began to have gazed looks and fixed attention in midair. Whatever had his attention was peaceful, calming and inviting because he was never scared or frightened. Zackie's experiences became interactive when he began to reach out in desire to become a part of what he was experiencing.

He would extend his weak, malnourished arms in the air like a child who wanted to be picked up. Reaching to be held because children know being held makes everything better. It was both beautiful and hard to watch. The beauty was in what I knew to be the innocent, spiritual longing and desire for Jesus and the sense of peace that accompanies that desire. The presence of death in our home made it hard to watch, but it wasn't scary. It was a peaceful and ministering spirit; the total opposite of what death is believed to be. I didn't want my son to die or the presence of death in our home, but Zackie was dying and death was there to transition him.

One Friday, the hospice nurse came to care for Zackie, it was July 25, 2014. It was exactly one month to the day that Zackie entered hospice care. As she was going through her care routine, she began to tell her funny stories. She would let Seth assist her as she told stories about her farm and the animals that lived there. Seth would hand her tape and bandages as he laughed at her stories; he felt good about helping her help Zackie. After she finished caring for Zackie and the stories ended, she calmly told me that she didn't think Zackie would make it through the night. I was so exhausted from fighting, and didn't know what to say or how to react to what the nurse had said. For a moment, I just sat with my eyes closed—waiting. I was waiting for my faith, strength and trust to recharge and kick in. My faith did recharge, my strength was renewed and my trust was still in God. I didn't want to hear or accept what she said. So, I told her she was wrong, Zackie was going to live and not die. God and His Word were all I had to stand on. So I didn't move my eyes from Him, I held firmly to hope and faith in God's promises.

At night the house would be very quiet, except for the oxygen machine; it made a loud, whooshing sound. After a while we got used to its rhythm and it became a part of the house's night sounds. On that particular night, July 25, 2014, the oxygen machine and its loud, rhythmic whooshing sound faded. Even though it was still pumping oxygen into Zackie's body, the whooshing sound faded into the background because Zackie was coding. His lips turned blue and he was unresponsive. All we could do is pray and ask God to help Zackie live, to help us not to lose our son.

God did help us. As we were praying, death loosened its grip. The blue in Zackie's lips faded away, his normal creamy complexion came back and he was breathing fine. That was a rough night, I can't explain it, but we weren't scared. We didn't have time to be scared. In life or death situations, your instincts take over. Instinctively, we knew to pray, and God saved him. Zackie didn't die that night, God kept him alive. Prayer—that was all we had. God heard our prayer and He answered.

Needless to say, but you don't sleep after an experience like that, the visual of Zackie dying is playing in your mind on repeat. The next couple of days weren't any easier than that night, the night Zackie almost slipped away. Zackie's body was being consumed by that greedy, insatiable tumor that was spreading all over his body. His tiny body was no match for the large, fast-growing tumor that was stretching out on the inside of Zackie like a tree's roots stretching deep into the dirt. The tumor began to push and press against Zackie's organs, as if to move them out of the way for its takeover. Deep blue and purple bruises and marks began to appear on his body due to the trauma going on inside of his body.

It was excruciatingly painful to watch Zackie's body deteriorate and not be able to help him or stop the unbearable pain he was in. All I knew to do was call on the Name of Jesus. My faith, trust, and confidence were in Him and His love and concern for Zackie and what we were going through. We absolutely had to have a peace that surpasses all understanding and a calm that kept us connected to Christ Jesus during those last days. It's the only way we made it to that point and prepared us for what would happen next.

LOVE AND LOSS

It was Friday, August 1, 2014. A week had passed since we almost lost Zackie. The day had gone by and the night had come. It happened again, Zackie began to slip away, but this time it was different than before. He was lying in his bed, dying. He was still breathing, but in a way that wasn't normal. His body was making a jerking movement similar to what a body does with hiccups. His lips didn't turn blue like before and this time he didn't come back when we prayed. We prayed, we shook him, we called his name, nothing, no response. All we could do was hold him in our arms and once more shower him with love and affection as he slowly transitioned from this world.

Tears were falling from our eyes, we didn't want this to be the end, we didn't want Zackie to die, we wanted a miracle. We continued to shake his body, call his name and pray, nothing, no response. I thought to touch the side of his neck to check his pulse; it was still there but it was weak and slow. I kept my hand on Zackie's pulse because it was the only indicator that he was still alive as his father held his lifeless body. After a few moments, Zackie breathed his last breath and I could feel his pulse no more. He was gone. I couldn't believe he was gone... I couldn't believe my son was gone. It was a peaceful transition, nothing parents should ever experience, but it was comforting to know that Jesus was there, in the room, to receive Zackie's spirit and usher him into heaven. There are no words to describe the pain we felt that night; it's so heavy it takes my breath away. We cried as we were still holding his lifeless body in our arms, but we couldn't fall apart and we couldn't give up, we had Seth and each other to care for.

This is the perfect place to encourage you to not get stuck at the intersection of death and living. Yes, mourn them, they are your loved ones. You loved them dearly and miss them terribly. I know I do; I miss my son. It deeply saddens me that Zackie is no longer here, but my husband and son are, and they need me to be present and available for them as I was for Zackie. After the death of a loved one, living without them can seem impossible, but that's only true if you decide to stay stuck—stuck at the intersection of death and living. Jesus loves you and desires to be in relationship with you, so receive Him today. By faith and trust in Jesus, you will see them again. So, decide to live, keep living, others are counting on your story and your testimony to help them get through losing their loved ones, as we hope our story has helped you.

It is absolutely amazing how fast a body turns cold after death—unbelievably fast. As I sat still holding Zackie's lifeless body, I could feel the cold creep in, pushing out the warmth that used to be a sign of life. His body began to stiffen and harden as his creamy complexion faded and the dull, blue grey look of death emerged. I was holding my son in my arms and he was dead, cold, stiff, and blue. I had no doubt God was with me, He is the only reason I could be in that moment and not completely lose my mind. God's grace held me together that night and I needed Him more than I ever did or probably will.

When someone passes away in hospice care you don't call 911, you call the hospice company. So, when Zackie passed away that's what we did, we called the hospice company to inform them our son had passed away. Their procedure was to contact Zackie's nurse and have her come to our home. During his transition, Zackie's body went through a lot. So, while we waited on the nurse, I cleaned his tired, worn-down body. I was feeling so many different emotions, but the two emotions I remember most were sadness and anger. I was sad because of the obvious, Zackie had just passed away. But the anger I felt wasn't directed at God, oh no, I knew better than to blame God for any bad that happens. No, I was angry at the greedy, insatiable tumor that ate constantly and consistently away at my son's body.

Honestly, while Zackie was going through the course of death, the tumor or cancer wasn't on my mind or in my thoughts. I was consumed with comforting my son during his transition.

The anger came after, when I witnessed my son's tummy that was inflated and stretched beyond comprehension, was now flattened to the normal size of a baby's tummy, but it was too late. I was angry because cancer had feasted on Zackie's body for ten months. Just spreading throughout his body; eating, surviving and growing from the blood in his organs. And when Zackie's heart gave out and there was no more blood to suck and live on, cancer and the insatiable tumor had gotten away with the death of my son. I was pissed. But, focusing on cleaning my baby's body for one last time, as I had done for days, weeks and months helped me remember that Zackie's earthly body may have been weak and worn, but his glorified body was perfect in heaven.

Zackie's nurse finally arrived, though sad for our family, she wasn't surprised Zackie was gone. Since there wasn't any care to provide, the first thing she did was call the coroner's office to report the loss of our son as an expected death. There were those words again, expected death. After a short conversation with the nurse, the coroner's office called Zackie's time of death, August 2, 2014 2:08 AM. According to the coroner, Zackie's death was official. During this traumatic experience I learned and grew a lot, but expecting my son to die was never one of the things I learned to do, nor will I ever.

Next, the nurse called the funeral home to request transportation for the remains of Zackie's body. While we waited, she stopped the dispensing of morphine and disconnected the IV tubing that carried the flow of morphine into Zackie's body. When the nurse disconnected the tubes, blood poured out from Zackie's port. Naively, I was surprised to see his blood because Zackie's nurse often told us his heart was working very hard to decide which organs to send the blood to. In that moment, at the sight of his blood, I remembered her saying Zackie's heart would eventually give out and that's how he would die. How does a healthy heart just give out? Her answer was one simple word, stress. When Zackie's heart had to decide which organs needed the blood most, the other organs started dying. That put an extreme amount of stress on his heart and in time it just gave out.

As I finished cleaning the blood from Zackie's body, the funeral home transportation arrived. In the early morning hours, two men had come to take my son's body to a cold, dark freezer. They wheeled the gurney into the foyer of our home. Respectfully, they told us to take our time and patiently waited in the background of the scene that was playing out in front of my eyes. We said our goodbyes and after some time placed Zackie's lifeless body on the gurney. The two men from the funeral home stepped out of the background ready to transport Zackie's body to the van waiting in our driveway. But before they took him away, I had to look at him again and kiss his cold, hard face one last time.

When the two men pulled the white sheet over Zackie's face, something broke inside of me. As Zackie's body left the foyer, the atmosphere had a feeling of finality to it. Zackie was gone never to return. The first time he had ever been out of the sight and care of his parents was when his dead body was on its way to a cold, dark freezer. That's what I was thinking in that moment. I just lost it and collapsed to the floor and cried, "God, please help me! O God, please help me!" I was completely and thoroughly exhausted; I literally had nothing left, but my God heard my cry and He helped me. I could feel strength, not my own, but a supernatural source of strength stirred up on the inside of me. I didn't know it then, but at that moment, I had survived the death of my son. God helped me get up from the floor that night; to be a wife to my husband and to help Seth understand his brother was gone, gone to heaven and one day we would see him again.

So much happened in those few hours—from the time of transitioning to the time of transporting—it seemed like a lifetime had passed. As hard and painful that traumatic experience was, I knew that we would be alright because God was undoubtedly with us just like He was with Zackie.

God was with us the entire time. We went through the hardest, most trying time of our lives, but we were never alone. The weight and pressure though seemingly crushing, was never able to overtake us because we were then and still is being held together by and in Christ Jesus. "

And He Himself existed before all things, and in Him all things consist, cohere, and are held together" (Colossians 1:17).

THE LAST DAYS – THROUGH A FATHER'S EYE'S
THE PROMISE AND THE FAVOR

When Zackie was diagnosed with cancer, suddenly, in an instant, God's charge and my promise became clear. At that moment, I understood what God asked of me. Instantly, I began to reflect on that October night when I was awakened by God with glad tidings of a son that was to be born. It was like reliving a story right out of the Bible—God telling Abraham when Isaac would be born or the angel Gabriel telling Zechariah when John would be born. I can remember it like it was yesterday; it was Wednesday October 24, 2012. During that time, my wife and I were in the process of adopting our second child and we were in our least favorite stage of the process—waiting to be selected. When God woke me, He gave me great news. God told me the set time and date that Zackie would be born. He also told me the day our case worker would call with the great news.

As God continued talking, He asked me to promise Him that I would take care of Zackie. I didn't understand why God asked me to promise because I take great pride in protecting and providing for my family. Everything I know about protecting and providing for my family I learned from my father, Ennis Antoine Sr. He was the best example of a man and father one could have. My mom and dad had seven kids and my dad was the sole provider for his family. Every day I watched him go to work in the morning and come home at night. He never complained or got angry or left his family. He was a good father; he provided for us and he was there for us. So, it was embedded in me that a man's responsibility is to protect and provide for his family. Yet God was asking me to promise Him that I would take care of Zackie.

Didn't He already know I would? God knows everything. He knows the number of hairs on my head and Psalm 139 verse 14 says, "I am fearfully and wonderfully made." Acts 17 verse 26 says, "God set the bounds of my habitation. He knew when and where I would be born and the parents I would be born to." Yet, on that October night He asked me to promise to take care of the precious child He was sending to us.

Of course my answer was yes. Providing food, clothes and a loving home was easy because it was natural to me. But, little did I know at that time, God had way more in mind than food or clothes. God knew Zackie would be diagnosed with cancer, He even knew Zackie would die at the young age of twenty one months. God knew Zackie needed an enormous amount of love, support and patience as he went through a grueling ten-month battle with cancer. God knew Zackie needed more than food or clothes, he needed my self-sacrifice and complete surrender to the promise. God also knew Zackie needed solace and a sanctuary of peace as he transitioned back to his Heavenly Father. God needed us to lovingly watch over Zackie during his battle and when the time came, wait with him, with heavy hearts as God received him back unto Himself.

Suddenly, it all made perfect sense when we took Zackie to his one-year appointment and I heard the doctor say Stage Four Liver Cancer. That's what God meant. This was the moment the promise was all about. All this time I thought I was fulfilling my promise to God by protecting and providing for Zackie. None of that was clear to me when God woke me that October night, but God knew the end from the beginning and what lied ahead of my life and the journey we were about to embark upon. Rarely does what God asks of us and what we understand it to mean are the same things. But, even in not telling us everything about what He is asking of us, His love is intricately weaving His plan for our lives, and, that plan almost always has to do with helping others. While you're doing His will, He never leaves you alone. He is right there with you carrying the load, making provision, providing favor, and rewarding your obedience. Remember, the reward for doing what He asks is always greater than what He asks of you.

Promise Me you will take care of him; those words came flooding back. As the loving Father He is, God knew this precious little boy would need a covering over him as he went through the hardest months of his young life. He needed someone to advocate for him and fight for him.

Fighting cancer would be an uphill battle, but I knew God was fighting for us as I would be for Zackie. As hard as that time was for me, my only reason for sharing this story is so you can understand the favor I asked God.

As time and the chemotherapy treatments went on, Zackie's cancer had spread and worsened. We decided to stop the treatments and place Zackie in hospice care. While in hospice, Zackie had some rough days, several times we almost lost him. Promise Me you will take care of him; I could still hear those words in my head. I believed God knew I had done everything I could to take care of and provide for Zackie. I knew Zackie was too special to God; his entire life was always in God's hands from the time he was born until what seemed like the end. So, if this was it, if God wasn't going to heal Zackie, I needed Him to do something for me. So, I prayed and asked God for a favor. The favor I asked God was based solely on the promise I made to Him concerning taking care of Zackie. I prayed, "Lord, I believe in You and trust You with my life, so if my son cannot be or will not be healed from cancer, promise me if he's coming to heaven with You, let his spirit leave this earth sitting in my lap and let him make his transition into Your lap." I literally wanted Zackie's spirit to go from my hands to God's.

THE MORNING

It's humbling how the day your son dies begins as a normal, routine day. It was Friday, August 1, 2014, a normal day for us, busy with lots of movement that was ordered by our daily schedule. The day went by fast as we took care of our daily needs, our six-year-old son, Seth, and Zackie who was very sick. After the busy day was over the night came and my wife was on Zackie-duty. We cared for Zackie in shifts and it was her turn that Friday night. For weeks and months we took turns checking on Zackie throughout the night, but this night was different, very different from how the day started. When she checked on him, he looked like he was in the process of dying because his breathing was different. My wife woke me up and said, "Babe, I think this is it." "What are you talking about?" I asked. At that moment it didn't dawn on me that she was talking about Zackie. It took me a minute to collect my thoughts and then it hit me, she was talking about our worst fear, Zackie was about to leave us. I quickly jumped out of bed and rushed into the living room where we had set up a care station for Zackie. He was barely breathing, my heart dropped, and all kinds of emotions flooded my heart.

I have never witnessed anyone dying before, let alone my son who I loved very much. It was surreal looking at my son leaving his world—that leaves a mark in your memory. I knelt down beside his bed and caressed him softly. I called his name, "Zackie, Zackie," hoping he would respond. He never said a word, he just laid there barely breathing. My wife called his name repeatedly, "Zackie, Zackie, Zackie," nothing, no response.

Without thinking, I picked him up and sat on the sofa and placed him in my lap. All I could think about was,

Lord, not today. As I sat on the sofa holding Zackie in my lap still hoping for a miracle, he took his last breath and passed away. I can't begin to explain the pain and hurt I felt as I checked his pulse to see if he was really gone. Zackie's face was so calm because his transition was peaceful. The last time I saw that peaceful look on his precious little face was when I would check on him in the middle of the night, and wonder like most parents, are you still breathing? But, this time he wasn't, he was gone.

Immediately, I became angry. I was so angry I could feel my blood boiling. I could not believe my precious son was gone. Did this just happen? Did my son just die? As I sat there holding my son's lifeless body in my arms, I was in disbelief and confused to no end. As the protector of my home, I was trying to wrap my mind around what just happened—Zackie was gone. Then it hit me, in the midst of the worst experience of my life, while my son's body became more and more stiff in my arms, God

fulfilled His promise to me. In that moment, I remembered the favor I asked God. I asked Him to promise me
that Zackie's spirit would go from my lap into His lap in
heaven. Wow! What an awesome God we serve. So, instead of focusing on Zackie's lifeless body in my arms, I
focused on the promise God made to me.

Understandably, my emotions got the best of me,
but my spirit revived quickly. Even though I was hurt
because of the transition of my son, it became apparent
to me that God fulfilled His promise. Although Zackie
wasn't delivered from cancer, he was delivered from a
body that was filled with cancer. Now, he is in a better
place. He can no longer come to me, but one day I will
go to him.

CONCLUSION

It is our desire that this book has encouraged you to keep fighting and hoping in the midst of a bad season in your life. We have learned so much on our journey *Between the Treatments*. Our strength and resolve were tested. Our faith was stretched and our patience was trialed, but through it all, we endured and grew. We can now look back over our journey and realize God was with us, and we grew closer because of it. Our family will never be the same again, but that's ok. We know that we're better, stronger, and wiser because of our journey *Between the Treatments*.

If this book has been a blessing to you, please consider sending us a testimony. We would love to hear from you.

You can send your testimony to: kwa@kwa.life

We've started a non-profit in our son's name to help those families that are going through similar challenges as we did.

It's called "Zachary Isaac Antoine Foundation." Please consider donating to help us in this fight.

Please visit: www.zia.life

PO Box 1295

Marrero, La. 70073

Zachary Isaac Antoine
FOUNDATION

Made in the USA
Columbia, SC
06 September 2020